Tennessee

MELISSA MCDANIEL

Children's Press®
An Imprint of Scholastic Inc.

Content Consultant
James Wolfinger, PhD, Associate Dean and Professor
College of Education, DePaul University, Chicago, Illinois

Library of Congress Cataloging-in-Publication Data
Names: McDaniel, Melissa, 1964- author.
Title: Tennessee / by Melissa McDaniel.
Description: New York, NY : Children's Press, an imprint of Scholastic Inc., 2019. | Series: A true book | Includes bibliographical references and index.
Identifiers: LCCN 2017060413 | ISBN 9780531235812 (library binding) | ISBN 9780531250945 (pbk.)
Subjects: LCSH: Tennessee—Juvenile literature.
Classification: LCC F436.3 .M352 2019 | DDC 976.8—dc23
LC record available at https://lccn.loc.gov/2017060413

Photographs ©: cover: Stephen Alvarez/National Geographic Creative; back cover bottom: Joe Fox/age fotostock/Superstock, Inc.; back cover ribbon: AliceLiddelle/Getty Images; 3 bottom: David Grimwade/Alamy Images; 3 map: Jim McMahon/Mapman ®; 4 left: MediaProduction/iStockphoto; 4 right: Ludmila Ivashchenko/Shutterstock; 5 top: Daveallenphoto/Dreamstime; 5 bottom: Juniors Bildarchiv GmbH/Alamy Images; 6 bottom: Raymond Gehman/Getty Images; 7 center: FRILET Patrick/age fotostock; 7 top: Sean Pavone/Shutterstock; 7 bottom: Mark Humphrey/AP Images; 8-9: Jon Bilous/Dreamstime; 11: Daveallenphoto/Dreamstime; 12: traveler1116/Getty Images; 13: RichardBarrow/Shutterstock; 14: rickberk/Getty Images; 15: Cynthia Kidwell/Shutterstock; 16-17: Malcolm MacGregor/Getty Images; 19: benkrut/iStockphoto; 20: Tigatelu/Dreamstime; 22 right: grebeshkovmaxim/Shutterstock; 22 left: Alexander Zavadsky/Shutterstock; 23 top right: megasquib/iStockphoto; 23 top left: Ludmila Ivashchenko/Shutterstock; 23 bottom left: MediaProduction/iStockphoto; 23 center right: Sieboldianus/Getty Images; 23 bottom right: Juniors Bildarchiv GmbH/Alamy Images; 23 center left: Tony Campbell/Shutterstock; 24-25: John Parrot/Stocktrek Images/Getty Images; 27: NativeStock/North Wind Picture Archives; 29: The Granger Collection; 30 bottom left: Nancy Carter/North Wind Picture Archives; 30 top right: Robert Lindneux/The Granger Collection; 30 top left: The Granger Collection; 30 bottom right: Alexander Zavadsky/Shutterstock; 31 bottom: Circa Images/Glasshouse Images/Superstock, Inc.; 31 top right: Bettmann/Getty Images; 31 top left: John Parrot/Stocktrek Images/Getty Images; 32: Bettmann/Getty Images; 33: Pictorial Press Ltd/Alamy Images; 34-35: F11photo/Dreamstime; 36: Cal Sport Media/Alamy Images; 37: Luc Novovitch/Alamy Images; 38: Luke Sharrett/Bloomberg/Getty Images; 39: Luke Sharrett/Bloomberg/Getty Images; 40 inset: bonchan/Shutterstock; 40 background: PepitoPhotos/iStockphoto; 41: Michele René/age fotostock/Superstock, Inc.; 42 top left: Charles Bird King/Glasshouse Images/Alamy Images; 42 top right: Barney Burstein/Corbis/VCG/Getty Images; 42 center: Science History Images/Alamy Images; 42 bottom left: Michael Olivers/Alamy Images; 42 bottom right: AP Images; 43 top: James McCauley/Alamy Images; 43 center right: DFree/Shutterstock; 43 center left: Tinseltown/Shutterstock; 43 bottom left: Ben Liebenberg/AP Images; 43 bottom right: Ronald Martinez/Getty Images; 44 bottom right: Kyle T Perry/Shutterstock; 44 top: Judy Eddy/WENN.com/age fotostock; 44 bottom left: almondd/Shutterstock; 45 top: Hal Stone/The Granger Collection; 45 center: Horizons WWP/TRVL/Alamy Images; 45 bottom: John Parrot/Stocktrek Images/Getty Images.

Maps by Map Hero, Inc.

Scholastic Inc., 557 Broadway, New York, NY 10012

1 2 3 4 5 6 7 8 9 10 R 28 27 26 25 24 23 22 21 20 19

Front cover: Spelunker in a Tennessee cave

Back cover: Downtown Nashville

Welcome to Tennessee

Key Facts

Capital: Nashville

Estimated population as of 2017: 6,651,194

Nickname: Volunteer State

Biggest cities: Nashville, Memphis, Knoxville

Find the Truth!

Everything you are about to read is true ***except*** for one of the sentences on this page.

Which one is **TRUE**?

T or F Many Civil War battles were fought in Tennessee.

T or F All of Tennessee lies within the Appalachian Mountains.

Find the answers in this book.

Contents

Raccoon

Great Smoky Mountains National Park

Tennessee walking horse

This Is Tennessee!

N
W
E
S
0
50
Miles

OHIO
INDIANA
WEST VIRGINIA
ILLINOIS
MISSOURI
KENTUCKY
VIRGINIA
ARKANSAS
NORTH CAROLINA
SOUTH CAROLINA
MISSISSIPPI
ALABAMA
GEORGIA
TENNESSEE
NASHVILLE
KNOXVILLE
MEMPHIS
CHATTANOOGA
Mississippi
Tennessee
Cumberland
Appalachian Mountains

1 Reelfoot National Wildlife Refuge
Tennessee National Wildlife Refuge
2 Country Music Hall of Fame and Museum
Tennessee State Capitol
Musicians Hall of Fame and Museum
World's Largest Guitar
Bristol Motor Speedway
Knoxville Zoo
Great Smoky Mountains National Park
4 Cumberland Caverns
3 Elvis Presley's Graceland
Sharpe Planetarium
Creative Discovery Museum
NASCAR SpeedPark

1 Reelfoot National Wildlife Refuge

This refuge protects Reelfoot Lake, Tennessee's largest natural lake, and the surrounding land. Visitors can go on guided tours to see eagles and other interesting birds.

MARYLAND

2 Country Music Hall of Fame and Museum

Nashville is the center of the country music industry. At the Country Music Hall of Fame and Museum, visitors can hear music by the most important country artists and see some of their instruments, gold records, and more.

3 Elvis Presley's Graceland

Rock-and-roll legend Elvis Presley lived much of his life in Memphis. Each year, more than half a million people visit his home, which is called Graceland. Visitors can explore Presley's mansion and see more than 20 of his cars.

4 Cumberland Caverns

Located in central Tennessee, Cumberland Caverns is one of the longest caves in the state. It features amazing rock formations and underground waterfalls.

ATLANTIC OCEAN

The Appalachian Mountains started forming about 480 million years ago

Land and Wildlife

Tennessee stretches long and skinny across the southeastern United States. It is divided into three major sections. East Tennessee is the section closest to North Carolina. It is mountainous. Middle Tennessee has rolling hills and many farms. West Tennessee is flat. The winding Mississippi River forms the state's western border.

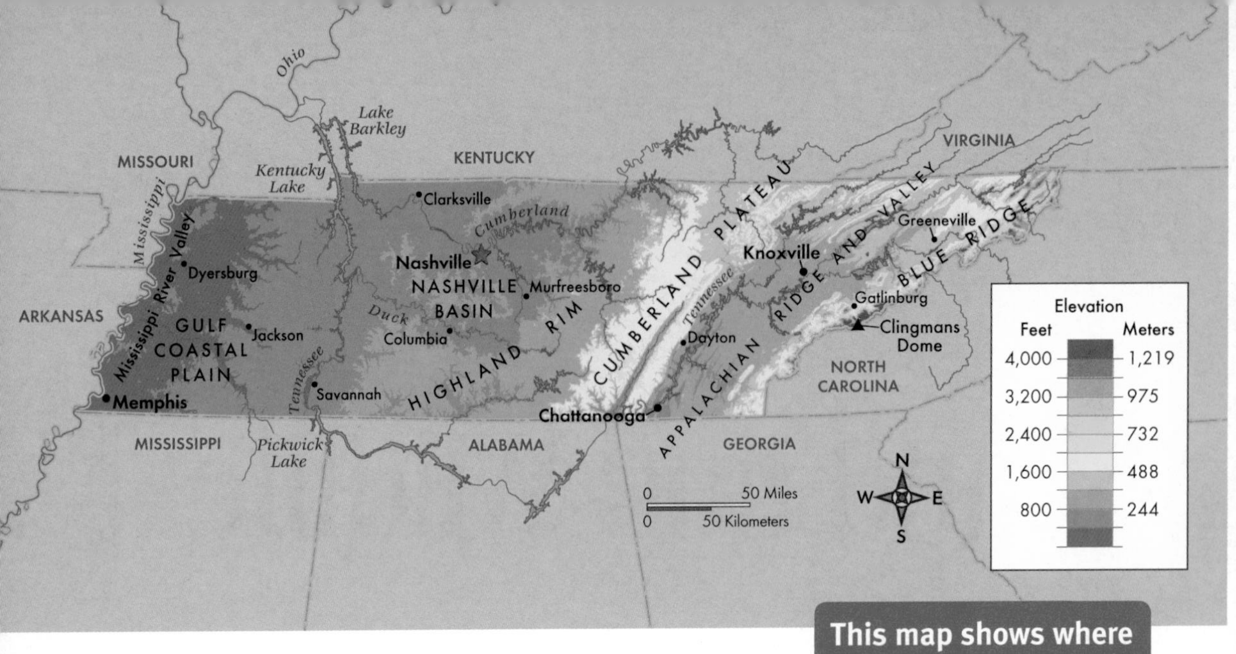

This map shows where the higher (red) and lower (green) areas are in Tennessee.

Mountains and Flatlands

East Tennessee is blanketed by the rugged ridges and narrow valleys of the Appalachian Mountains. This ancient mountain chain extends all the way from Canada to Georgia. In Tennessee, the mountains are marked by forested ridges and steep valleys. In the past, the rough land made travel through the region difficult. In Middle and West Tennessee are farms where crops such as cotton, soybeans, and flowers grow.

Great Smoky Mountains National Park

Great Smoky Mountains National Park stretches from eastern Tennessee into North Carolina. This mountainous park is covered in forestland. Its woods are home to thousands of types of plants and animals, ranging from wild **boars** to wild turkeys. This amazing scenery draws huge crowds of tourists, making Great Smoky Mountains National Park the most visited national park in the country.

In recent years, air pollution has become a problem in the area. The whitish haze from cars and power plants has reduced the park's gorgeous views.

Great Smoky Mountains National Park gets its name from a natural mist that settles along its ridges.

Rivers and Lakes

Rivers have long been a vital part of Tennessee's landscape. Swampy wetlands line parts of the Mississippi River in the west. These wetlands teem with wildlife. The most important river in the east is the Tennessee. It once flooded frequently. Beginning in the 1930s, a series of dams was built to control flooding and make electricity. These dams created many lakes. One of them, Kentucky Lake, is one of the largest **reservoirs** in the country.

The Tennessee River flows in a U shape that spans much of the state.

Snow blankets a wooded park area in Nashville.

Warm and Wet

Tennessee has a mild climate. Winters are cool, and summers are warm. The weather is generally warmer in the western part of the state, where summers can be hot and sticky. In winter, snow blankets the eastern mountains, but snowfall is rare in the west. It rains a lot everywhere in the state. Thunderstorms are common, and they sometimes bring huge chunks of hail.

Natural Colors

Tennessee's rich forests are often bursting with color. In spring, the creamy-white blossoms of dogwood trees stand out brightly against deep-green leaves. In summer, rhododendron and azalea shrubs bring splashes of pink and purple to the forests. The leaves of trees such as beech, hickory, and walnut turn shades of copper and gold in autumn. In the swamps of West Tennessee, majestic cypress trees stay green throughout the year.

In fall, many people like to drive along Newfound Gap Road to see the changing colors of the leaves in Great Smoky Mountains National Park.

About 6,000 black bears live in Tennessee.

Amazing Animals

The forests of eastern Tennessee are home to an amazing array of animals, from bears to bobcats to bats. Birds make music in the treetops. Woodpeckers tap their rhythms on trunks while warblers sing pretty tunes. The state's waters are also alive with life. Along lakeshores, herons stand quietly in the shallow water, waiting for insects to appear. In deeper water, loons dive for fish and frogs. Meanwhile, catfish move along river bottoms, feeding on whatever they find.

Tennessee's capitol was designed to look like an ancient Greek temple.

CHAPTER 2

Government

From 1796 until 1812, Knoxville served as the first capital of Tennessee. But the city's location in rugged East Tennessee made it hard for people to reach. So the capital was moved first to Nashville and then to Murfreesboro. Both cities are more centrally located. The small town of Kingston became the capital for a single day in 1807 when state lawmakers met there to fulfill a **treaty** with the Cherokee people. Finally, in 1843, Tennessee's legislators voted on where the capital should be permanently located. They chose Nashville.

State Government Basics

Tennessee's government has three branches. The executive branch is led by the governor. It runs the government and carries out state laws. The legislative branch makes laws for the state. It consists of the Senate and the House of Representatives. The state courts make up the judicial branch of government. These courts settle disputes and hold trials for people charged with crimes.

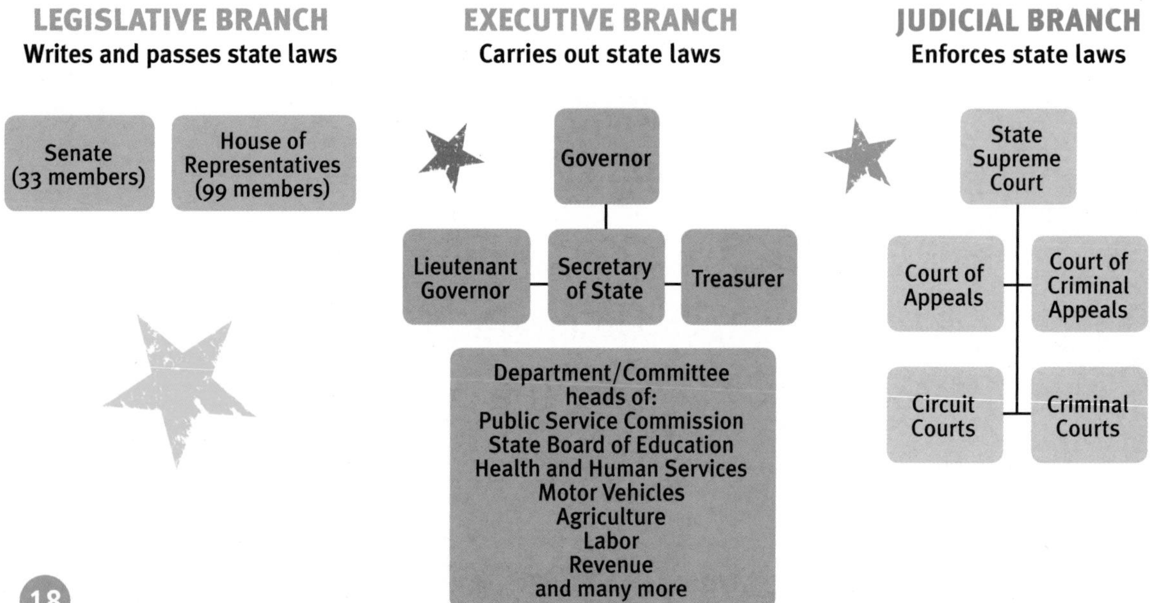

The Constitution

A constitution is a document that describes the structure and rules of a government. Tennessee's first constitution was created in 1796, the year Tennessee became a state. At the time, Tennessee had few people, and the constitution created a small government. It did not even include a state supreme court! The Tennessee constitution has been replaced twice since then. It has also been amended, or changed, many times. In 1978, it was amended to allow a governor to serve two terms in a row.

Local police departments are overseen by city and county governments.

Tennessee in the National Government

Each state elects officials to represent it in the U.S. Congress. Like every state, Tennessee has two senators. The U.S. House of Representatives relies on a state's population to determine its numbers. Tennessee has nine representatives in the House.

Every four years, states vote on the next U.S. president. Each state is granted a number of electoral votes based on its number of members in Congress. With two senators and nine representatives, Tennessee has 11 electoral votes.

With 11 electoral votes, Tennessee's voice in presidential elections is averag compared to other states.

The People of Tennessee

Elected officials in Tennessee represent a population with a range of interests, lifestyles, and backgrounds.

Ethnicity (2016 estimates)

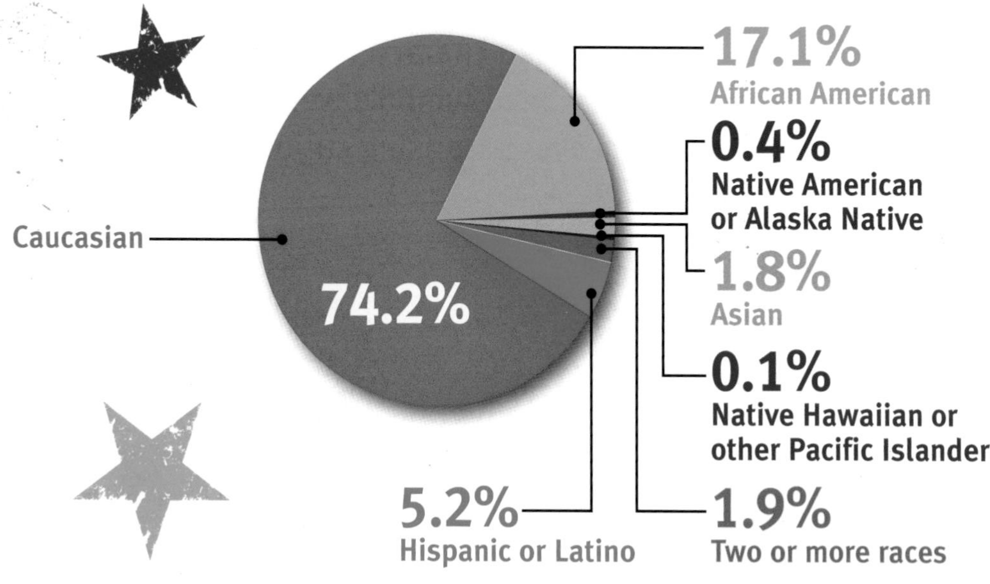

67% own their own homes.

5% were born in another country.

25% have a bachelor's degree or higher.

86% of the population graduated from high school.

7% speak a language other than English at home.

What Represents Tennessee

States choose specific animals, plants, and objects to represent the values and characteristics of the land and its people. Find out why these symbols were chosen to represent Tennessee or discover surprising curiosities about them.

Seal

Tennessee's state seal shows a plow, wheat, and a cotton plant. These indicate the importance of agriculture to the state. Below these symbols is a boat. It represents the importance of trade along the state's rivers.

Flag

The state flag contains three white stars in a blue circle against a field of red, with a blue stripe on one side. The stars represent Tennessee's eastern, central, and western regions.

Passionflower

STATE WILDFLOWER

Found throughout the South, this flower has a ring of frilly purple fibers above creamy-white petals.

Eastern Box Turtle

STATE REPTILE

The eastern box turtle can pull its head and limbs all the way inside its shell and close its shell tightly. This helps protect it from **predators**.

Tulip Poplar

STATE TREE

The tulip poplar was named the state tree because it grows all across Tennessee. Pioneers often used its wood to build houses and other buildings.

Mockingbird

STATE BIRD

Chosen as the state bird in 1933, the mockingbird is famed for its ability to copy the calls of other birds.

Raccoon

STATE WILD ANIMAL

The raccoons found in Tennessee measure about 30 to 38 inches (76 to 97 centimeters) long, including their tails. They weigh about 12 to 25 pounds (5 to 11 kilograms).

Tennessee Walking Horse

STATE HORSE

First bred in Tennessee, this horse is known for its calm personality and smooth ride.

More than 10,000 soldiers on each side died during the Battle of Shiloh during the Civil War (1861-1865).

History

People have lived in what is now Tennessee for thousands of years. Early people gathered plants for food and hunted giant creatures such as **mastodons**. By about 10,000 years ago, people started growing food. They raised squash and sunflowers. More than 1,000 years ago, the Mississippian culture developed. These people formed huge mounds of earth and built temples on top. They also lived in large cities. Thousands of Mississippian people lived in a settlement called Mound Bottom in Middle Tennessee.

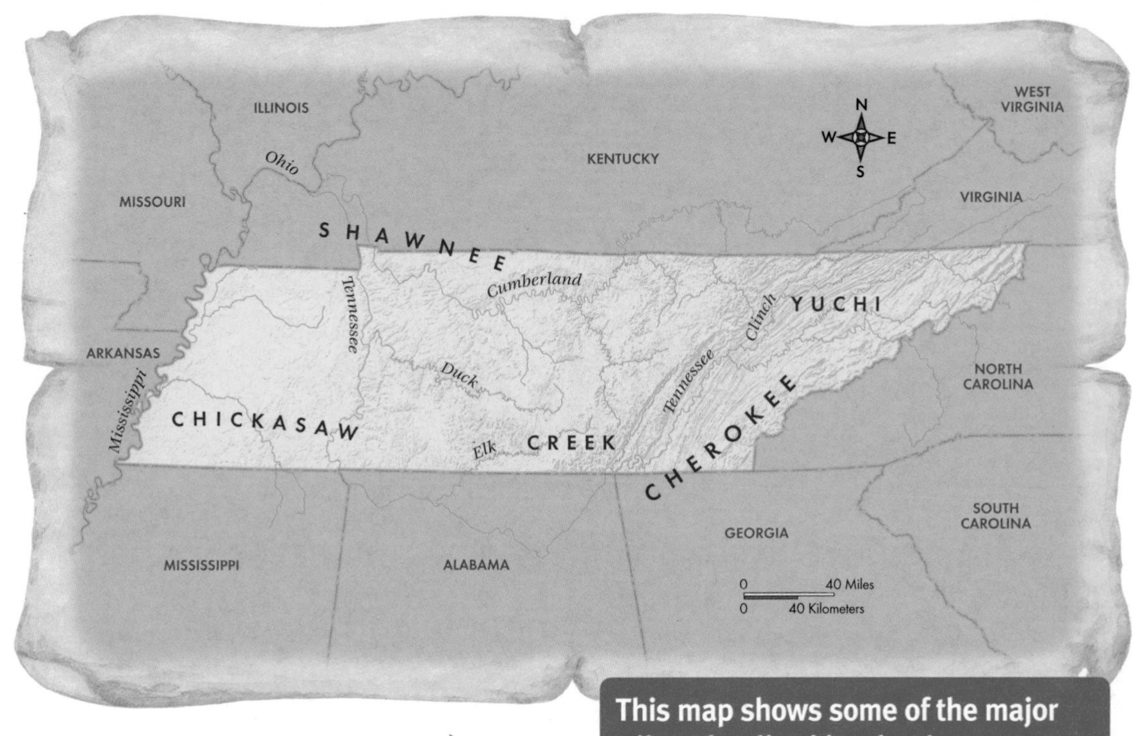

This map shows some of the major tribes that lived in what is now Tennessee before Europeans came.

Many Cultures

In the 1400s, the Mississippian culture disappeared. It was replaced by a number of smaller Native American groups. The Creek settled in Middle Tennessee, while the Chickasaw people lived to the west and the Yuchi and Cherokee to the east. These people all hunted, fished, and farmed. Their main crops were corn, beans, and squash.

Cherokee built homes by weaving branches and bark together and using dried mud to hold everything in place.

In the Village

Tennessee's Cherokee people lived in villages of about 200 people each. They fished, hunted, and grew crops such as corn, beans, and squash.

In summer, Chickasaws lived in rectangular houses. The houses had triangular, tented roofs that were open at the front and back. The roofs kept the rain out but allowed breezes to pass through easily. This made the houses cooler inside. In winter, people would move to sturdier round houses. These wooden houses were coated with clay. This kept the wind and rain out during the chilly weather.

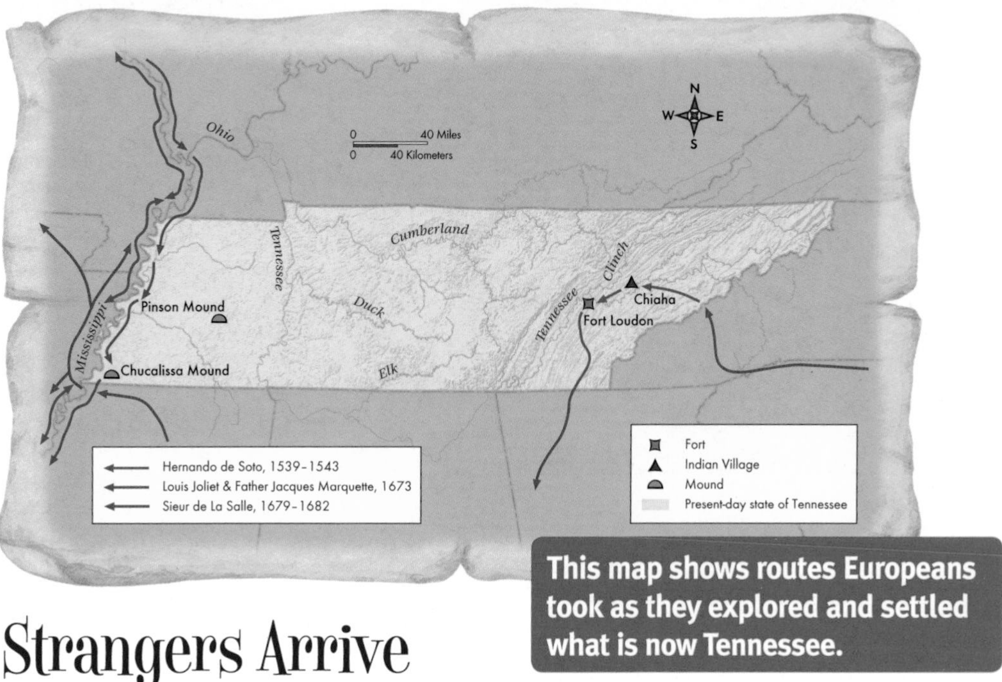

This map shows routes Europeans took as they explored and settled what is now Tennessee.

Strangers Arrive

The first Europeans to arrive in Tennessee were searching for gold. Spaniard Hernando de Soto led a group into the region in 1540. He found no riches. Later Spanish explorers were also disappointed. In 1673, Frenchmen Jacques Marquette and Louis Joliet sailed down the Mississippi River. They were interested in trading with Native Americans. Other French settlers followed. They built forts and trading posts where they traded guns, blankets, and other goods for furs.

Settlers From the East

Around the same time, English explorers began making their way across the rugged Appalachian Mountains from the East Coast to Tennessee. They set up trading posts and began building settlements. By the time the American Revolution began in 1775, a few thousand white colonists lived in the region. After the revolution, Tennessee was part of the new state of North Carolina. In 1796, it became a separate state.

Before exploring North America, Hernando de Soto took part in the conquest of Peru and much of Central America.

The Trail of Tears

White settlers often battled with the Native Americans for control of the land. The Creeks were forced to give up much of their land following the Creek War (1813–1814). Then, in the 1830s, the U.S. government began forcing Native Americans to move west. In 1838, Cherokees and others were forced to march to what is now Oklahoma. Thousands died on this Trail of Tears.

The Civil War

Meanwhile, tensions were growing over the issue of slavery. It had gradually been outlawed in the North but was widespread in the South. When the Civil War (1861–1865) began, most Tennesseans were loyal to the Union. However, the state sided with the proslavery **Confederacy**. Many battles were fought in Tennessee. By the time the Union won the war in 1865, Tennessee was in ruins.

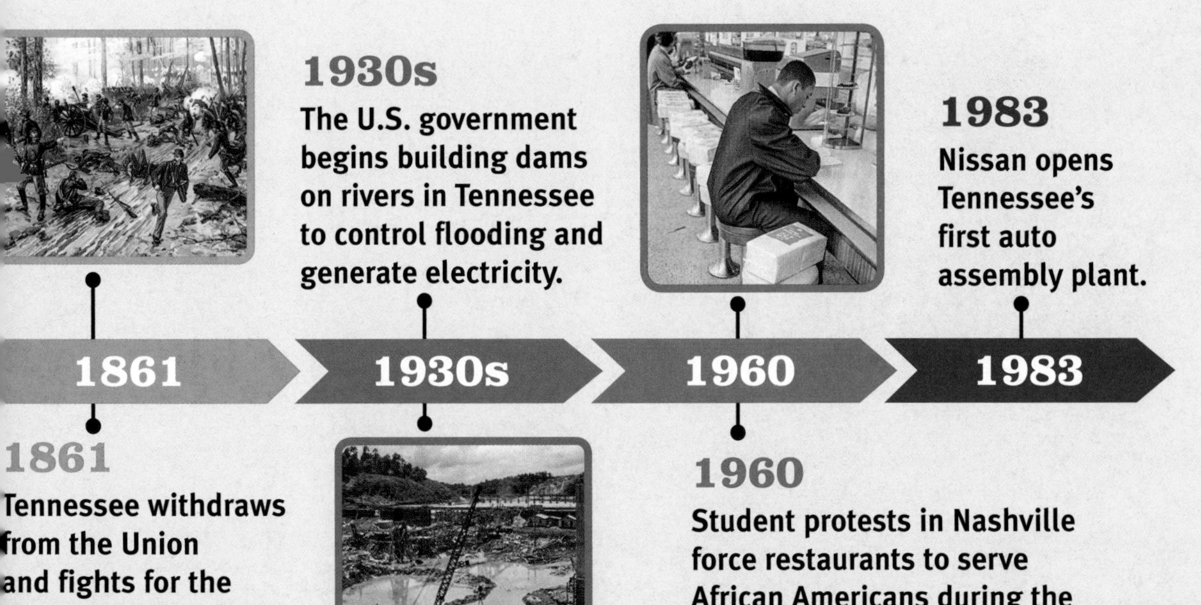

1861
Tennessee withdraws from the Union and fights for the Confederacy during the Civil War.

1930s
The U.S. government begins building dams on rivers in Tennessee to control flooding and generate electricity.

1960
Student protests in Nashville force restaurants to serve African Americans during the civil rights movement.

1983
Nissan opens Tennessee's first auto assembly plant.

The Civil Rights Movement

Even after the end of slavery, **segregation** was common throughout the South. Black and white people went to separate schools, sat in separate waiting rooms, and drank from separate water fountains. During the civil rights movement of the mid-20th century, African Americans led the fight against this system. In Nashville, black students began **sit-ins** at restaurants that served only white people. After months of protests, Nashville became the first major city in the South to begin to undo segregation.

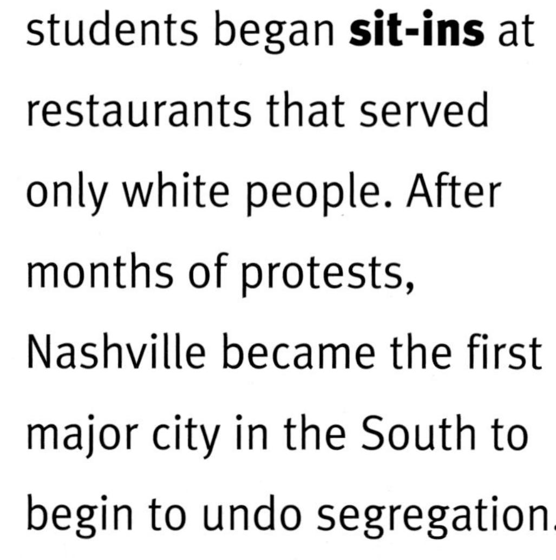

Protesters in Nashville and other Tennessee cities used sit-ins to call attention to the unfair treatment of black people.

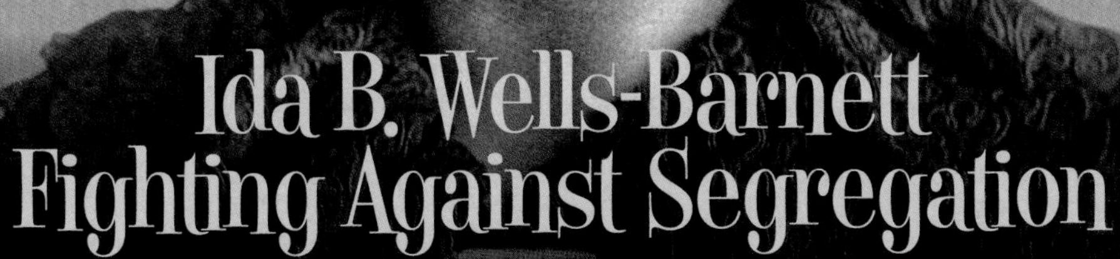

Ida B. Wells-Barnett Fighting Against Segregation

Ending segregation required brave acts by many thousands of people. One of them was longtime Memphis resident Ida B. Wells-Barnett. In 1884, Wells-Barnett refused to give up her seat in a whites-only section of a train. A few years later, she began editing the *Memphis Free Speech* newspaper. Wells-Barnett used her position to challenge segregation. She also became a leader in the fight against lynching, a practice where white mobs murdered black people after accusing them of crimes. Wells-Barnett continued the fight for civil rights until her death in 1931. She was also a major inspiration for later civil rights leaders.

Sun Studio is often called the birthplace of rock and roll.

Culture

Music is the heart of Tennessee. For more than 100 years, powerful blues music has poured from clubs along Beale Street in Memphis. Memphis has also produced fantastic soul and rock music. Early rock icons such as Elvis Presley and Roy Orbison recorded hits at the city's Sun Studio. Memphis's Stax Records produced soul musicians like Otis Redding and Carla Thomas, while Nashville has long been the worldwide center of country music.

Sports Fans

Tennesseans love sports. In Nashville, fans cheer for the Tennessee Titans football team and the Nashville Predators hockey team. In Memphis, basketball is a favorite. Fans root for the Grizzlies. The University of Tennessee women's basketball team is legendary. The Lady Volunteers have won eight national championships. Pat Summitt was their coach for 38 years. During this time, she led the team to 1,098 wins, more than any other coach in college basketball history.

The University of Tennessee Lady Volunteers are known simply as the Lady Vols to fans.

Bluegrass musicians perform at the Smithville Fiddlers' Jamboree, an annual music and craft festival in the small town of Smithville.

Celebrating Tennessee

Many Tennessee events celebrate the state's musical heritage. Fantastic fiddlers and other **bluegrass** musicians show up at the Smithville Fiddlers' Jamboree and Crafts Festival. Bluegrass, jazz, and blues bands play at the Riverbend Festival in Chattanooga. A different part of the state's heritage is celebrated at the National Storytelling Festival in Jonesborough. People come from all over the world to tell and listen to stories.

FedEx's fleet of cargo planes is the largest in the world, with more than 650 airplanes.

At Work

Tennessee was once an agricultural state. Far fewer people work on farms today, but some still grow crops such as corn and cotton. Others raise chickens or cattle. Many more people go to work in factories. They build things such as cars and computer parts. Zinc, copper, and coal are dug from the ground. Services also play a large role in the Tennessee economy. FedEx, one of the nation's largest delivery services, is based in Memphis.

Workers install parts on an assembly line at the Nissan plant in Smyrna.

Wheels of Progress

Tennessee does not have nearly as many manufacturing jobs as it did at the end of the 20th century. But the car industry is booming. In 1983, the Japanese company Nissan became the first automaker to build a plant in Tennessee. Today, it is one of the state's largest employers. More than 130,000 people work in the auto industry in Tennessee. Cars and trucks are now among the state's most valuable **exports.**

Let's Eat

Tennesseans love to eat barbecue and fried catfish. Many meals include corn bread or hush puppies, which are fried balls of cornmeal. Meals often come with sides such as mac 'n' cheese or collard greens. For dessert, diners might enjoy a slice of gooey pecan pie.

Corn Bread

Ask an adult to help you!

This tasty dish goes well with just about any meal. Try it alongside barbecue or enjoy it by itself!

Ingredients

1 cup cornmeal
1 cup flour
1 tablespoon baking powder
$\frac{1}{4}$ teaspoon salt
$\frac{1}{4}$ teaspoon baking soda
1 tablespoon sugar
$1\frac{1}{4}$ cups plain yogurt
1 egg
$\frac{1}{4}$ cup vegetable oil

Directions

Preheat the oven to 375°F. Combine all the dry ingredients in a bowl. In another bowl, mix the yogurt, egg, and oil. Combine the wet and dry ingredients. Stir them together so there are no dry parts, but do not stir too much. The mixture should be lumpy. Pour it into a pie pan greased with butter. Cook for about 24 minutes, or until the top starts to brown. Serve warm.

Plenty to See and Do

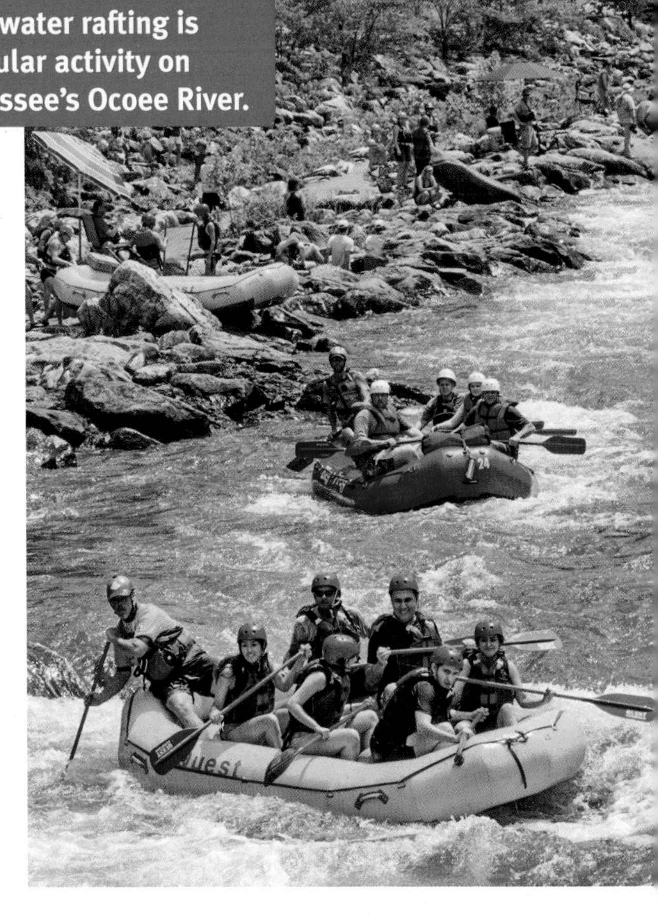
Whitewater rafting is a popular activity on Tennessee's Ocoee River.

Tennesseans are proud of their friendly nature. Whether you're visiting Tennessee from out of state or you've lived there your whole life, they would love to show you their favorite parts of the state. You can ride a roller coaster or ride a horse through fields. You can explore caves and climb mountains. You'll also want to check out some music. Whether you like country or blues, rock or hip-hop, you'll be sure to hear some great tunes. There's something for everyone in Tennessee! ★

Famous People

Sequoyah

(ca. 1775–1843) was a Cherokee leader who grew up in Tennessee. As a young man, he developed a system of writing for the Cherokee language. Before that, it was solely a spoken language.

Davy Crockett

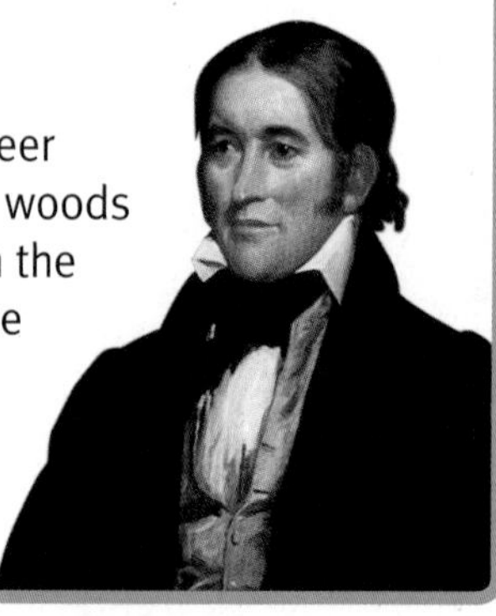

(1786–1836) was a legendary pioneer and politician who was born in the woods of eastern Tennessee. He served in the state legislature and the U.S. House of Representatives before going to Texas to fight for independence from Mexico. He died in the famed Battle of the Alamo.

Bessie Smith

(1894–1937) was one of the greatest blues singers of all time. She had a rich, powerful voice and a spellbinding performance style. She was from Chattanooga.

Tina Turner

(1939–) is a rock and soul singer from Nutbush. Her raw energy and gritty voice sent songs such as "Proud Mary" and "What's Love Got to Do With It" to the top of the charts.

Wilma Rudolph

(1940–1994) was a runner who became the first American woman to win three gold medals in a single Olympic Games. As a child in Tennessee, she had polio, a disease that often makes patients unable to walk. After years of therapy, she overcame her disability. By high school, she was a star athlete.

Dolly Parton

(1946–) is a country music star who has won nine Grammy Awards. She is from a poor part of East Tennessee. She wanted to help the area's economy. In 1986, she purchased a stake in an amusement park in the region and turned it into a theme park called Dollywood. The park has rides and traditional music and crafts. It attracts more than 3 million visitors a year.

Samuel L. Jackson

(1948–) is an actor from Chattanooga. He has appeared in more than 150 movies, including *The Avengers* and *Jurassic Park*.

Reese Witherspoon

(1976–) is an actor who grew up in Nashville. She won an Academy Award for her performance in *Walk the Line*.

Justin Timberlake

(1981–) is a singer and actor from Memphis. He has sold millions of records, both as a solo artist and with the group NSYNC. He has also starred in movies such as *The Social Network*.

David Price

(1985–) is an All-Star Major League pitcher. In 2012, he won the Cy Young Award for being the best pitcher in the American League. He is from Murfreesboro.

Did You Know That . . .

Nashville's Grand Ole Opry has broadcast a live radio show every weekend since 1925. No other live radio program has been running as long.

More people visit Great Smoky Mountains National Park than any other national park in the country. Each year, about 10 million people visit the park to hike and take in the views.

The Great Smoky Mountains are sometimes called the Salamander Capital of the World. About 24 species of these amazing amphibians live in the park.

Tennessee is called the Volunteer State because so many Tennesseans volunteered to fight in the Mexican-American War (1846–1848).

The Peabody Hotel in Memphis is famous for its ducks. The birds spend their day in a fountain in the lobby. At the end of the day, they march across the carpet to the elevator. They ride it to the roof, where they spend the night.

Did you find the truth?

T Many Civil War battles were fought in Tennessee.

F All of Tennessee lies within the Appalachian Mountains.

Resources

Books

Herman, Gail. *Who Was Davy Crockett?* New York: Penguin, 2013.

Rozett, Louise (ed.). *Fast Facts About the 50 States: Plus Puerto Rico and Washington, D.C.* New York: Children's Press, 2010.

Somervill, Barbara A. *Tennessee.* New York: Children's Press, 2015.

Stone, Omar. *Chickasaw.* New York: PowerKids Press, 2016.

Visit this Scholastic website for more information on Tennessee:

 www.factsfornow.scholastic.com
Enter the keyword **Tennessee**

Important Words

bluegrass (BLOO-gras) a type of country music, typically played on banjos and guitars

boars (BORZ) wild pigs with tusks

Confederacy (kuhn-FED-ur-uh-see) the group of 11 states that declared independence from the rest of the United States, prompting the Civil War

exports (EK-sports) products sold to another country

mastodons (MAS-tuh-dawnz) huge extinct mammals related to elephants

predators (PRED-uh-turz) animals that live by hunting other animals for food

reservoirs (REZ-ur-vwahrz) natural or artificial lakes in which water is collected and stored for use

segregation (seg-rih-GAY-shuhn) the act or practice of keeping people or groups apart

sit-ins (SIT-inz) protests in which people sit in restaurants or offices and refuse to leave until their demands are met

treaty (TREE-tee) a formal written agreement between two or more warring parties

Index

Page numbers in **bold** indicate illustrations.

About the Author

Melissa McDaniel is the author of more than thirty books for young people. She was born in Portland, Oregon, and attended both Portland State University and the University of Washington. She now lives in New York City, where she works as a writer and editor.